"In this touching book, Ginger Farry takes us into her class-room and introduces us to her students. You'll find yourself smiling as the author prays in rhyme for The Chatter Bug, The Sunshine Girl, and Mr. Looney Tune. This teacher takes great pains to know her students. In the Challenger, she sees past a child's anger: 'She's scared deep inside, yes, I know this is true, and the anger is a front that I just can't break through.' For teachers this book will be a comfort and a joy. It's a great gift book."

Judy Esway
Author, *Real Life, Real Spirituality* and *Letting Go*

"Ginger Farry prays well from both sides of the teacher's desk. Let her words fan the embers of your own teaching experiences of students lost in love, joy, boredom, pain, or silence. Then fill your eyes with the specks and flashes of God's presence in the faces of those you teach."

John J. Boucher
Training Director, Charism
Diocese of Rockville Centre

"I well recall the times when, at the end of a school day, I dropped to my knees in the chapel and asked the Lord for the grace of some slight clue as to what made one or anoth-er of my students lovable. Their lovableness was sometimes far from obvious to me. Ginger Farry's *A Teacher's Prayerbook* reflects such days in the life of a religious educator and/or teacher of adolescents. Yet it also reflects the glory days, the days when we are touched by innocence, openness, and goodness in the youth we meet. Her prayers for teachers also ring true. They are an honest appeal for the survival skills that only God's grace can supply."

Pamela Smith, SS.C.M.
Director of Lay Ministry Programs
SS. Cyril and Methodius Seminary
Orchard Lake, MI

"Insightful, powerful, touching, and inspiring. A must-read for every teacher. This unique collection of prayers are joyous and hopefilled and may even bring a tear to the eye. Ginger Farry has performed an immensely valuable service in creating this powerful spiritual resource for teachers. It provides a variety of prayers that can breathe new life into the weary in spirit. It is a wonderful invitation to go deep within and experience a profound communion with your students in the heart of God. I recommend it highly!"

Bridget Mary Meehan
Author, *God Delights in You*

"Ginger Farry is a person who has a real enthusiasm for life, teaching, and people. I especially enjoyed reading her book because I could feel myself agreeing with her over and over. She has a knack for being able to pinpoint so many things that we teachers face, day in and day out. Sometimes it might only be looking forward to that break between classes, a few shared words with a colleague that gives you that needed lift, or simply getting the right seating plan and being able to say a heartfelt, 'Thank you, God.'"

Sr. Theresa McDermott, OP
Language Teacher
Harbor of Grace Convent, College Point, NY

Dedication

This book is dedicated to all those who teach, most especially my colleagues at Msgr. McClancy Memorial High School and to my old friends at Agnes Academic School, and particularly to:

Mr. Nardone, Ms. Gendron, Ms. Mallia, Ms. Guzzo, Mr. Porro, Mr. Pinto, Sr. Nancy Farry, Sr. Marianne Miller, Mr. Rescigna, and to the memory of one of God's finest, gentlest teachers, Sr. Maureen Troike.

—*Ginger Farry*

Acknowledgments

My thanks to my friend and colleague Kathy Ryan for her invaluable input, encouragement, and for several prayers within this book. Whenever we came together for discussion and/or just simple conversation, both the book and I ended up the better for it.

My thanks also to two very special brothers of the Sacred Heart. First, to my principal, Brother Joseph Rocco, whose consistent praise and encouragement is always a constant reminder of God's love, and to Brother Robert R. Croteau whose inspiring suggestions for additional prayers opened up many new spiritual doors.

—*Ginger Farry*

Twenty-Third Publications
185 Willow Street
P.O. Box 180
Mystic, CT 06355
(860) 536-2611
800-321-0411

ISBN 0-89622-727-8
Library of Congress Catalog Card Number 97-60131
Printed in the U.S.A.

Part One: For Our Students

Part Two: For Us, the Teachers

A Teacher's Prayerbook

Introduction

We all know that a good student/teacher relationship is important if we are to teach our students in any meaningful way. And sometimes, as we attempt to move students to a deeper understanding of themselves, they challenge us to an ever stronger commitment to care.

Frequently, however, there is not enough time or energy in the day to get to know every student, let alone learn his or her story. (Those who teach religion only once a week have an even more difficult task.) How do we get to the essence of each child and situation? How do we remain focused on the individual, mold and shape future seekers and dreamers, and empower them to grow to full promise—while concentrating on the demands placed upon us by curriculum, grades, extra activities, and discipline?

I believe that in order to communicate with students on a heart level, God must be invited into the dialogue. In order to single out any situation that brings us to joy, gratitude, tears, anger, questioning, self-discovery, or a sense of pride, it seems necessary to "pray the day anew," reflecting on what is at the core of each experience. That is how the prayers here came to be. Each was inspired by a particular student whose life touched a teacher in a way that was disturbing, sensitizing, or beautiful. Each student was prayed for, thought about, and described in a journal. Many of these students were mine, some belonged to my colleague and friend, Kathy Ryan, but now we hope that they will be recognized by you as "yours" as well.

Following each of these "For Our Students" prayers are brief reflections and sometimes questions for you to ponder in relation to your own students.

Also in these pages are prayers for teachers, for days (and classes) we are afraid might never end, for Mondays that came too fast and went too slow, for the times we didn't want to pray and just couldn't feel any love at all. These prayers chronicle the good and bad days, the ups and the downs, the joys and the disappointments in the life of a teacher. There are no reflection questions with these because the prayer *is* the reflection.

I invite you to join me in prayer. And, as you do, I hope that you will reflect and share with God the trials, the troubles, and the triumphs of your own teaching life, whether you are a full time teacher or a volunteer catechist.

May we all give praise to the Master Teacher.

Part One

For Our Students

He's in a Huff

His eyes were made small by anger,
his lips formed a constant smirk.
He seldom brought his book to class
or indulged in any work.

And when I sent him from the room
my prayer seemed so absurd,
that he'd unclench his tightened fists
and someday hear your Word.

Reflection

It is not always easy to look beyond the anger in a
student and see through to the fear.

Think about the last student in whom you saw anger
recently, and imagine what he or she might be fright-
ened about.

On the Fence

She's wavering on the brink, Lord,
    she can't make up her mind.
One day she prays in earnest,
    the next, she will decline.

I know that she's been hurt, Lord,
    and the fear is always there,
that if she gives herself to you
    she won't be "anywhere."

So she holds on to opinions
    and her intellect so wise
while emotions run the gamut
    from anger and tears to sighs.

Help her, Lord, with understanding,
    let her see that it is "cool"
and that giving all to you, Lord,
    makes her the wisest fool.

Reflection

I pray this child will learn how to let go and put things in your hands. Indeed, I put her there right now.

- Is there a student like this in your class?
- What is your prayer for him or her?

The Noisemaker

He makes noises in my class, Lord,
  he's silly and a pest.
He yells at all the others,
  thinks he's better than the rest.

Sometimes, he is deceitful,
  sometimes, he seems sincere.
O, Lord, I give this child to you.
(Because I really don't want him here!)

Reflection

Sometimes we feel affection for a student, even when
he or she tries our patience. Sometimes we feel no
affection at all.

•Is there a child in your class for whom you cannot
feel love? Pray about feeling God's love for this student.

He's Likeable, Lord

He's one of my favorites,
    though I couldn't say why.
It's not that he's brilliant
    because he simply "gets by."

It's not that he's good
    or handsome or quiet.
Yet I love when he says:
    "Hey, teacher, I'll try it."

Reflection

Thank you, Lord, for children who do their best, no matter what their best may be.

- Is there someone in your class who always tries hard?
- Do you let him or her know how proud you are of their efforts?

The Chatter Bug

Today this child said she hated me, Lord,
   as I sent her from the room.
And though I was angry she'd talked on a test,
   I might have reacted too soon.

This impetuous youngster just can't keep still,
   her lips move in constant chatter.
Oh, how can I teach her silence, Lord,
   when to her life's a "talking" matter?

And indeed, she needed to have the last word
   as she approached the door,
   like a child so filled with hurt who screams
   "I don't love you anymore."

I may have missed the boat with her,
   I need your guidance now.
Let her talk, and let me listen,
   O, Lord, please show me how.

Reflection

• Have you ever reacted too quickly to a difficult situation?

• Would you have reacted differently if you had waited and prayed?

Surprised by Faith

This youngster's bright and quiet
   and as manly as can be.
He never lets the others see
   his sensitivity.

But just today
   while we all prayed,
   my eyes flashed on his face.
And when he threw a kiss to you,
   dear Lord, I felt your grace.

Reflection

Thank you, Lord, for allowing me to glimpse this student's faith. Please continue to enrich it as today he enriched mine.

•Is there a child in your class who enhances your faith?

He's Number One

His will is all important, Lord,
not yours, not mine, just his.
He needs to be top dog, the boss,
even though he is no wiz.

He struts around like Number One,
while something inside smolders,
and I can feel the burdens, Lord,
he carries on his shoulders.

Reflection
• Is there a student in your class who seems to carry a lot of burdens? How do you handle this? Say an extra prayer for this child today.

The Challenger

*T*he mouth on this child, Lord,
  is hostile and loud.
And she loves to challenge
  each face in the crowd.

She's scared deep inside
  yes, I know this is true,
and the anger is a front
  that I just can't break through.

But I'll try every day
  with new hope and a prayer
to reach for her pain
  and to listen and care.

Reflection

How can I mirror your love for a difficult child, Lord?

• Is there someone in your class you can't reach?

• What ways have you tried?

Mr. Looney Tune

I'm afraid, Lord, that he's crazy,
he's charming yet disturbed.
He sings under his breath in class,
and echoes my every word.

I've kept him after school a lot,
and he'll always apologize.
And when I talk to him of you,
there's a glimmer in his eyes.

I can't tell if I've made progress
or if he'll ever right his wrongs.
Because he still sings in my class, Lord,
but now they're religious songs.

Reflection

Lord, it strikes me that sometimes a child needs
nothing more than to know that someone is listening
and someone cares. Help me to be that someone.
Help me to reflect your love.

Mr. Unpopular

*T*hey don't like him, Lord,
    and I'm not certain why.
They pick on him so,
    I could almost cry.

He studies a lot
    and his marks are good, too.
But they call him a "nerd,"
    so I guess that's a clue.

And they laugh when he speaks
    and poke fun at his walk,
and they tell lies about him
    though I know it's just talk.

Yet there's more to their pranks,
    it's a hate they're revealing.
So please help this child cope, Lord,
    you know what he's feeling!

Reflection
• Is there a child in your class that others pick on?

• What can you do to alleviate this situation? What would Jesus do?

• Have you ever reflected on the pain this student might be feeling?

A Teacher's Joy

She's quiet and respectful
 with a faith that's strong and true.
She writes me little notes, Lord,
 about her faith in you.

And even if she never leads
 your people as a "preacher,"
 she'll be a gentle witness
 and a gift to every teacher.

Reflection

What (or who) are some of the "joys" of teaching for
you? Make a list and hold it out to God in thanksgiving.

He's Beginning to Know You...

You are new to him, Lord,
   though he's not new to you,
and he shines with your love,
   everlasting and true.

What a joy that he's found
   the way and the light.
Help him stay on the path;
   help him fight the good fight.

And when, Lord, he stumbles,
   as all of us do,
reveal your compassion
   and mercy too.

Reflection

Help me, Lord, to do my part in showing this child
how to grow in you.

• Is there a child in your class on the verge of discovering his or her faith?

• How can you help without being intrusive?

Humble Us, Lord

He knows the subject well, Lord.
His grades are very high.
But yet he is a challenge
   and I'm sure that you know why.

He's self-assured and confident
   there's nothing he would hide,
   but Lord he lacks humility—
   this fellow's filled with pride!

He chuckles when the others fail,
   he just has no compassion.
And I have had to fight myself
   in almost the same fashion.

Because when he is so unkind,
   I want to strike back, too,
   but the way to teach him gentleness
   would be to act like you.

The only way to show this child
   that kindness is the key,
   is to let him see humility,
   mirrored today in me.

Reflection
How do you want me to handle a bully, Lord? Help
me not to "bully" back.

•How do you handle students who test your patience
and love?

Later, Lord

She just isn't ready
for faith's biggest lurch.
It's on the back burner
(like going to church!).

A commitment is something
you make with a guy,
not with a God
who's up in the sky.

O, Lord, let her see
you're not far away,
and help her to know you
starting today.

So the next time she speaks,
your mercy, don't hide,
and show her you live
right there inside.

Reflection

•Do you have a student whose priorities are all mixed up?

•How can you assist in helping her or him fix them?

"A" for Effort

She's one of the sweetest,
I can't help but express
that I like that she tries
and passes each test.

Though her grades are just average,
her spirit's an "A,"
and she follows you, Lord
so please light up her way!

Reflection

•Is there a child that lights up your classroom,
though his or her grades are mediocre?

•What can you do to let this child know how special
he or she is?

This Child
Is Troubled

This child is troubled,
    he's confused and he's lost.
And I hear that his family
    has paid quite a cost.

Though they wanted to help him,
    they now live apart,
    and still bicker and quarrel
    'til it just breaks his heart.

He'll say that he's dumb,
    and acts wild as a loon,
    but he's bright and he's sad
    and he needs some love soon.

As he tells me with glee
    what he did to his cat,
    I can't help but ask him:
    "Why did you do that?"

And he laughs and retorts,
    "I don't like him, you see,
    so what's the big deal,
    just like they don't like me."

And I know in my heart
why he wanted to maim
because deep down inside,
he holds all the blame.

O, Lord, heal his hurt
and help him to grow
and learn of your love
so the past he'll let go.

Reflection

•Is there a child in your class who is hurting or who always needs attention? How do you handle this?

•Have you brought this child to prayer?

A Thankful Achiever

He doesn't reveal a lot, Lord,
but he does well in my class.
Without a doubt, he studies,
and certainly, he'll pass.

But what I like about him most
is that everyday in prayer,
when I ask for some intentions,
he puts his family there.

Reflection
Thank you, Lord, for children who are thankful.
• Is there someone in your class who inspires you and helps you keep hope in your heart?

The Sunshine Girl

I love the way she loves you, Lord,
    puts all things in your hands.
I love the way she prays, Lord
    (she's one of your biggest fans!).

She's trusting and accepting,
    she gives you all her fears,
    so openly and joyously
    (and sometimes through her tears).

And such enthusiasm
    must surely help the rest.
Dear Lord, I thank you for this child,
    for her sparkle and her zest.

Reflection
•Is there a student who images God's smiling face for
you? Remember to thank God for him or her.

He's So Good in the Hall

One moment it's "Good morning,
  how's everything today?"
"How nice of you to ask,"
  I simply smile and say.

But then the bell resounds
  and the "niceness" just goes walking,
  as I request and finally bellow:
  "Will you please stop talking!"

Reflection
• Is there someone in your class who cannot sit still
and listen? What do you do?
• How do you help this child find the "peace" within?

He Thinks I'm His Mother!

He'll ask me for a tissue,
  he sometimes "takes" my pen.
At lunch he needs a dollar
  (I feel like Mother Hen).

He's always so uncertain
  if he's ready for the test.
He'll come and ask for special help
  and admit that he's a pest.

The truth is, Lord, he is a "noodge"
  who can't stay in his seat,
  but even in his helplessness,
  he's really rather sweet.

But, Lord, I do have one request,
  before his goose I cook,
  please have him give me back my text—
  that rascal took my book!

Reflection

• Is there a student in your class who tries to make a "mother" out of you?

• How can you help her or him grow?

Parent/Teacher Talk

His parents came up to school today,
  and they want to know where they went wrong.
They said that they've tried
  and tried, and tried;
  it was a familiar song.

And I just didn't have the answers, Lord,
  for surely these parents care.
So I counseled them with, "Don't lose heart—
  just put your hope in prayer."

Reflection
•What do you tell the parents of a problem child?
•Do you suggest praying with them?
•Do you pray *for* them and their child?

Too Silent

She's ever so quiet, Lord,
   she sits by herself all day.
She never joins the others,
   she has nothing much to say.

She stares at empty spaces;
   she's locked up deep inside.
If only I could find the key,
   O, Lord, you know I've tried.

Don't let her fall between the cracks,
   for I hear her silent plea.
I was quiet, too, dear Lord,
   until a teacher talked to me.

   —Kathy Ryan

Reflection

Help me, Lord to find the right words so that this child can respond.

• Is there someone you can't reach, someone who's lonely and left out? What are you doing about it?

Just Listen...

"I'm wired today,"
  she said with a grin.
"I just can't sit still,
  can't settle in."

"What's charging you up,"
  I smiled and said.
"What kind of stuff
  is clogging your head?"

"My Mom's very cranky,
  my Dad has the flu,
  my dog just had puppies,
  an art paper's due.

"My Grandma is coming,
  I'm cut from the team,
  my best friend is moving,
  I just want to scream!"

I listened and listened,
  and let her have her say,
  'til she blew me away with:
  "Thanks, now I'm okay."

—Kathy Ryan

Reflection

Sometimes our students really need someone to talk to.
Give me discernment, Lord, about when to "just listen."

Losing It

I called a kid a fool today
  which wasn't the thing to do.
It only became clear to me
  when he called me a fool too.

I said a silent prayer for help,
  O, Lord, what should I say,
  and suddenly inspired,
  I was shown the way.

I said, "I'm very sorry, son,
  for what I said to you."
He paused and then he looked at me
  and said, "I'm sorry, too."

—Kathy Ryan

Reflection

Help me, Lord, with my own imperfections as a teacher. Help me to see them more quickly and to correct them as well.

•Have there been times when you said or did something you immediately regretted? What did you do?

Mr. Invisible

He loves to chat before class begins
and tell me where he's been,
and where he's going.

And sometimes I'll ask him questions
and he'll always have
a bright retort.

But as soon as he hears the sound of the bell,
he turns away and sits at his desk
in utter silence.

And I wonder what happened...
to the friendly, earnest fellow
who liked to talk.

Reflection
•Is there a child who can talk to you but doesn't
speak a word in front of the group?
•How can you encourage his or her participation?

Thank You for Him, Lord

He's a perfect young man,
   respectful and smart.
He's quiet and gentle,
   he speaks from the heart.

But I'm prejudiced, Lord,
   (since I heard from his brother)
   that he's telling his friends
   I resemble his mother!

Reflection

Thank you, Lord, for the children who make this job of mine easier. Strengthen me to be patient and kind with those who make my job difficult.

Yakety Yak

She's just about always talking,
  she never comes up for air,
  she interrupts each lesson,
  I know she doesn't care.

Her notebooks are all empty;
  her homework is never done.
And all she ever talks about
  is are we having fun?

I know I just don't get it,
  the "Valley Girl" display,
  but maybe I should listen, Lord,
  to what she has to say.

  —Kathy Ryan

Reflection
• Do you have a child that is not in the least interested in learning?
• How do you begin to touch her or him?

I'm Not Sure about Him...

I can't tell what he's thinking,
I can't read him at all;
   is this boy sincere?
I can't make the call.

Some days he will laugh
   at the wrong time and place.
Is it me that he's mocking?
Or am I just off base?

And sometimes he seems
   so earnest and proud;
   then I notice this smirk
   right before he gets loud!

But mocking or honest,
   this boy's worth a mention,
   though others have problems
   that need more attention.

Reflection

Help him, Lord, to learn to be sincere. Help me to be compassionate and allow me to see him through your eyes.

Friendless

How much he wants to be like all the others
   frolicking and acting tough and cool.
And yet he's not accepted by his brothers,
   and he doesn't seem to have a friend at school.

So he hangs out at my desk and asks me questions
   about the weather and about the time.
And I can see the loneliness within him.
O, Lord, please bless this child of yours
   —and mine.

Reflection
• Is there someone in your class who is always alone?
• Do you try to help by including him or her in group projects?

She Cheated...

She cheated, Lord,
and I don't know why,
and when I asked
she began to cry.

Then something inside me
led me to say,
"We won't talk about this
after today."

And the crying stopped,
but her face she hid,
"It won't happen again, ma'am."
And it never did.

Reflection
• Are you as a teacher more "just" or more "merciful"?
• Are there times when you could be less judgmental?

Daughter of Divorce

She acts just like we're friends, Lord,
She smiles and says, "What's up?"
I know she needs a friend, Lord,
*   because her parents just broke up.*

I want to be there for her,
*   her grades are getting low,*
*   I'm reaching out and praying—*
*   I don't know how far to go.*

Be with her, Lord, and guide her,
*   and help me show her too,*
*   it isn't "me" she needs, Lord;*
*   this child's in need of you.*

Reflection

• Are you aware of the personal or family problems your students are experiencing?

• Do you ever ask?

• Do you pray for students with personal problems?

Teacher's Pet

She calls herself my "favorite," Lord,
    and it's quite clear to see
        that through her many struggles,
        she has attached herself to me.

And I give her my attention
    after class and after school,
    and she'll say to all the others,
    "See, this teacher thinks I'm cool."

But I know her heart is heavy
    because her burden isn't light.
She watched her father die, Lord,
    and prayed both day and night.

And her brother had some trouble
    and they sent him far away,
    and still she prays to you, dear Lord,
    every night and day.

And though some think that she is strong
    I know that isn't true.
All the strength she musters up
    is sent her, Lord, by you!

So bless her, Lord, and keep her safe,
And please help her to know,
that though you have no favorites,
you'll never let her go.

Reflection

Help me, Lord, to be sensitive to the needs of my students. Help me to think of them as "whole" persons—not just as "students" in my class.

So Much Pain

She lost her mother;
he lost his dad,
so very young,
so very sad.

I gave them prayer cards
and a note,
and I went to the wake,
but words stuck in my throat.

O, Lord, please bless them,
and show them you care,
and help them to know
that you're always there.

Reflection

Help me to be sensitive and caring, Lord. When there's nothing I can do, please watch over my students as only you can.

Part Two

For Us, the Teachers

No Two Are Alike

Each class is different;
it's easy to see
the change in
personality.

Some are solemn
and just no fun,
though quiet is a blessing
when day is done.

Some have spirit
and seem alive,
and their joy prevails
and gives me drive.

Yes, some are good
but there's one that's not,
and every day—
I dread this lot.

Alone each kid
might be a chore,
but together indeed
there's mischief in store.

So help me, Lord,
*   I know you can,*
*   and show me the way*
*   to a good seating plan!*

Time for a Break

*T*omorrow is a holiday,
and you know what that means.
They're antsy and they're eager
(and they're bursting at the seams).

I don't want to yell or shout;
I'd like to play it cool.
Let's face it, Lord, we all can use
a day away from school.

So help me mellow out today,
please listen to my knock—
'cause I can't get their eyes on me
while they're staring at the clock.

It's Been a Wonderful Day

*T*hank you, Lord,
   for a wonderful day.
Everyone worked
   and there was time for play.

They laughed with me
   in "creative" time
   and I know that they learned
   and it felt sublime.

So thank you again
   for this smoldering ember.
If tomorrow is tough
   I'll have today to remember!

God Bless Weekends

It's Friday, my Lord,
and there's joy in the hall
from the faculty room
to the lunchroom and mall.

And we're all looking forward
to Saturday and Sunday
with prayers in our hearts
to be ready for Monday!

I Need a Different Outlook

I need a different outlook, Lord,
there are still four months to go,
and February's dragging
and we've had a lot of snow.

And looking at their faces,
I see they're tired too.
They could use a change, my Lord,
they need something new.

So please inspire me, dear God,
before the March winds blow
to lighten up their hearts (and mine)
so time won't move so slow!

I Don't Love Them Today

I don't love them today,
   I don't love them at all;
   they're feisty and noisy,
   they're just off the wall.

And I don't have the patience
   I have to admit,
   They've gotten to me
   and I'm in a snit.

But I know that you care, Lord,
   they're part of your plan,
   so I give you them NOW,
   just do what you can.

The Generation Gap

I'm afraid I need assistance, Lord,
with their vocabulary.
Do I really understand them?
Their jargon can be scary.

I'm "teacher," I'm not "yo" or "dude"
    on this I do insist,
    and "crowd" is out but "posse" is in
    on their current list.

And "word" means "truth," I've come to know,
    but "cool" is still okay,
    and I don't know if it's "hep" or "hip"
    that is acceptable to say.

I blundered just the other day,
    I called a fellow "buster,"
    and the class convulsed in laughter
    for this word has lost its luster.

Please help me, Lord, keep up-to-date,
    on meanings, right and true,
    because anything can change, Lord,
    except my faith in you!

Walk With Them, Lord

Bless them, Lord,
the big and small.
Guide them too,
each one and all.

Help them, Lord,
to learn and grow.
Heal them and
please let them know
that your love and mercy
won't go away
so enlighten them, Lord,
day by day.

Help Me, Guide Me

I'm teaching a new topic, Lord
(though it's not new to me).
I want to make it very clear,
    as clear as it can be.

So guide me and direct me, please,
    and help me with my fears,
    and one more thing, dear Jesus,
    please OPEN UP THEIR EARS!

Setting Priorities

My plan book is waiting;
exams are piled high,
   the grades are due Thursday,
   time is just flying by.

There are calls to return
   from two moms and my son,
   my prep is now over
   and nothing seems done.

There's a kid in the hall,
   and she's troubled, you see,
   and she wants to talk
   to no one but me.

But there goes the bell,
   and today's class can't wait;
   since I'm being observed
   and I just can't be late.

O, Lord, help me focus,
   prioritize now;
   let me live in this moment,
   please show me how.

"Meet me at lunch, dear,
   hang in for awhile,
   I'll have time then to listen,"
   I say with a smile.

And her eyes become brighter
   and she smiles her okay
   and I touch her shoulder
   as I walk away.

And inside my heart,
   I say a small prayer,
   "We both need your help, Lord,
   but I know you'll be there."

          —Kathy Ryan and Ginger Farry

Every Day Is Different

Sometimes, Lord,
    I can breeze through the day,
    joyous about my profession
    and happy that
    I teach.

Sometimes, Lord,
    I bungle it by losing patience,
    wallow in frustration
    and question why
    I'm here.

Most times, Lord,
    I accept my failures,
    come to you for renewed strength
    and rejoice…
    that you—and June—
    are never far away.

Open to Change

Open us, Lord,
keep us open to change,
to develop our insight
and broaden our range.

To begin anew
when we're lacking with fire,
and give us the grace
to rise up from the mire.

Stretch us, O Lord,
beyond where we are,
though it causes discomfort,
help us follow your star.

For no one can grow
and no one can gain
unless first we look at
our places of pain.

A Day of Grief

A student died today, Lord,
and all of us prayed.
We prayed together,
not as a school
but as a family,
holding tightly
to our faith.

It was a sad day and yet
we all pondered
if in heaven,
a choir of angels sang
while a ray of golden light
brightly welcomed
another star.

A Heartfelt Prayer

Bless us, O Lord,
in all our chores
from sharing knowledge
to erasing boards,
from marking tests
and quizzes as well,
and handing them back
'till the sound of the bell.
From figuring grades
with lightning speed,
and meeting with parents
to settle each need.

Deliver us, Lord,
from anger and tears,
from nasty cracks
and occasional jeers,
from endless days
and meetings that bore,
from paperwork
and memos galore,
from rainy mornings
when their eyes are closing,
from trying to teach
when they seem to be dozing.

Inspire us, Lord,
*   with faith and with hope,*
*   and gift us with patience*
*   to help us cope.*
And show us the way
*   that's both right and true,*
*   to win them over*
*   just for you.*
So fill us, dear Lord,
*   with your spirit and grace,*
*   'til in every child*
*   we can see your face.*